BUSINESS COST CONTROL SYSTEM 2024

STRATEGIES, CASE STUDIES AND INNOVATIONS

BY

EDEN WALKER

2024

BUSINESS COST CONTROL SYSTEM

Strategies, Case Studies, and Innovations:

EDEN WALKER

Contents

Chapter 1: Introduction

Imagine navigating through the intricate landscape of business operations, where every decision carries a price tag. In this dynamic environment, understanding and controlling costs become paramount for sustainable success. Chapter 1 sets the stage by delving into the fundamental concepts of Business Cost Control, exploring its significance and laying the groundwork for a comprehensive journey into effective cost management.

1.1 Overview of Business Cost Control

Cost control, at its essence, involves managing and optimizing expenditures within an organization. It encompasses a strategic approach to minimize expenses while maximizing efficiency and value. To illustrate, consider a manufacturing company that identifies raw material costs as a significant portion of its expenses. Through diligent cost control measures, such as negotiating bulk purchase discounts or seeking alternative suppliers, the company can effectively reduce its raw material expenditure without compromising product quality.

In this context, understanding cost drivers becomes crucial. Differentiating between fixed and variable costs provides a foundation for businesses to tailor their cost control strategies. For instance, fixed costs like rent remain constant regardless of production volume, while variable costs, such as direct labor, fluctuate with output. Armed with this knowledge, businesses can develop targeted cost control initiatives tailored to specific cost components.

1.2 Importance of Cost Management in Business

The importance of cost management extends far beyond mere financial considerations. It acts as a linchpin for strategic decision-making, influencing everything from pricing strategies to investment decisions. Take, for example, a technology startup aiming to launch a new product. By meticulously managing development costs and production expenses, the company can determine an optimal pricing structure that aligns with market expectations and ensures profitability.

Moreover, effective cost management enhances organizational agility. In a rapidly changing business landscape, companies must adapt swiftly to stay competitive. Through proactive cost control, businesses can allocate resources more efficiently, fostering the flexibility needed to respond to market shifts and emerging opportunities.

Cost management is not a one-size-fits-all endeavor. Tailoring strategies to align with organizational goals and industry dynamics is essential. A service-oriented business, for instance, might focus on optimizing labor costs and improving productivity, while a manufacturing entity may prioritize supply chain efficiency and production costs.

In practice, renowned companies exemplify the transformative power of cost management. Toyota, a pioneer in lean manufacturing, revolutionized the automotive industry by implementing efficient production processes that minimized waste and costs. By continually refining their cost control strategies, Toyota maintained a competitive edge and set industry benchmarks.

In summary, this Chapter provides a panoramic view of Business Cost Control, emphasizing its critical role in shaping organizational success. From understanding the basics of cost control to recognizing its far-reaching implications, this chapter serves as a primer for the in-depth exploration that follows.

Chapter 2: Fundamentals of Cost Control

In the intricate tapestry of cost control, Chapter 2 unravels the fundamentals that form the backbone of effective cost management. We delve into the nuanced understanding of costs, explore the dynamics of cost-volume-profit analysis, and categorize costs based on their behavior. Through practical examples, we illuminate these concepts, showcasing how businesses can navigate the complex terrain of cost control.

2.1 Definition and Types of Costs

Defining Costs:

Costs represent the monetary value of resources consumed to achieve a specific purpose. It's imperative to distinguish between explicit costs (direct, measurable expenses) and implicit costs (opportunity costs, not directly incurred but still impactful).

Types of Costs:

1. **Fixed Costs:** These remain constant regardless of production levels. For instance, rent for a production facility.

2. **Variable Costs:** Fluctuate with production volume. Examples include raw materials and direct labor.

3. **Semi-Variable Costs:** Exhibit characteristics of both fixed and variable costs. Utilities, partly fixed and partly variable, are a typical example.

Practical Example:

Consider a software development company. Fixed costs may include office rent and salaries of permanent staff, while variable costs involve expenses tied to project-specific needs, like additional contract developers. Understanding these cost types enables the company to allocate resources effectively, ensuring optimal budgeting for both ongoing operations and project-specific requirements.

2.2 Cost-Volume-Profit Analysis

Understanding CVP Analysis:

Cost-Volume-Profit (CVP) analysis assesses the interplay between costs, sales volume, and profitability. It aids decision-makers in determining the impact of changes in production levels or pricing on overall financial performance.

Key Components:

1. **Fixed Costs and Contribution Margin:** Fixed costs remain constant, while the contribution margin (selling price minus variable costs) contributes towards covering fixed expenses.

2. **Break-Even Point:** The point where total revenue equals total costs, signifying neither profit nor loss.

3. **Margin of Safety:** The difference between actual sales and the break-even point, providing a cushion against unexpected downturns.

Practical Example:

Imagine a retail business contemplating a price increase. CVP analysis helps assess the impact on break-even points and potential profits. If the increase doesn't significantly affect sales volume, the business can boost profitability without a substantial rise in costs.

2.3 Cost Behavior and Classification

Cost Behavior Patterns:

Understanding how costs behave under varying conditions is crucial for effective cost control. Costs can exhibit fixed, variable, or mixed behavior.

Fixed Costs Behavior:

Remain constant irrespective of production volume or sales. Rent and salaries often fall into this category.

Variable Costs Behavior:

Directly tied to production levels. As production increases, variable costs rise proportionally.

Mixed Costs Behavior:

Combine elements of both fixed and variable costs. For example, a utility bill might have a fixed monthly charge and a variable component based on usage.

Practical Example:

Consider a restaurant. Fixed costs may include monthly rent, while variable costs encompass ingredients for dishes. As the restaurant expands, fixed costs remain steady, but variable costs increase with higher demand. Recognizing these patterns allows the restaurant to adjust pricing and control costs effectively.

In essence, this Chapter unveils the intricacies of cost control fundamentals. From defining and categorizing costs to leveraging CVP analysis and understanding cost behavior, businesses can utilize these insights to make informed decisions that drive financial success.

CHAPTER 3: COST CONTROL STRATEGIES

In the ever-evolving landscape of business, Chapter 3 takes a deep dive into strategic approaches for effective cost control. We explore budgeting and forecasting as proactive tools, delve into the nuances of activity-based costing, analyze variance to identify deviations from plans, and introduce the principles of Lean Six Sigma in cost control. Practical examples will illuminate how businesses can implement these strategies to optimize their operations and financial outcomes.

3.1 Budgeting and Forecasting

Budgeting Overview:

Budgeting serves as a proactive financial roadmap, outlining expected revenues and expenses over a specific period. It enables businesses to set financial goals, allocate resources efficiently, and monitor performance against predefined benchmarks.

Forecasting Significance:

Forecasting complements budgeting by predicting future trends and uncertainties. It involves analyzing historical data and market conditions to make informed estimations. By integrating forecasting into budgeting, businesses enhance their adaptability to dynamic environments.

Practical Example:

Consider a retail chain planning its annual budget. Historical sales data, coupled with market trends, informs revenue projections. Operational costs, such as inventory and staffing, are meticulously budgeted. If a forecast indicates a potential surge in demand during a specific season, the business can adjust its budget to accommodate additional inventory and staffing needs.

3.2 Activity-Based Costing

Understanding Activity-Based Costing (ABC):

Activity-Based Costing allocates indirect costs to specific activities, providing a more accurate representation of how resources are utilized. Unlike traditional costing methods, ABC identifies the true cost drivers within an organization.

Key Components:

1. Identifying Activities: Break down operations into discrete activities, such as production setups or customer service.

2. Assigning Costs: Allocate indirect costs to activities based on their consumption of resources.

3. Calculating Activity Rates: Determine the cost per unit of activity to accurately assign costs to products or services.

Practical Example:

Imagine an automobile manufacturer using ABC to analyze production costs. Instead of allocating overhead costs uniformly across all products, ABC reveals that the setup and production changeovers for certain high-performance models incur higher indirect costs. This insight allows the company to refine pricing strategies and optimize resource allocation.

3.3 Variance Analysis

Variance Analysis Overview:

Variance analysis compares actual financial outcomes to budgeted or expected results, identifying discrepancies and deviations. It provides actionable insights into the reasons behind financial performance variations.

Types of Variances:

1. *Revenue Variances*: Analyzing differences between actual and expected revenues.

2. *Expense Variances:* Examining variations in operational expenses and identifying cost overruns or savings.

3. *Profit Variances:* Assessing overall profit differences compared to projections.

Practical Example:

Consider a software development project. If the actual development costs exceed the budget due to unforeseen challenges, variance analysis helps pinpoint the specific areas contributing to the overrun. This allows project managers to adapt strategies, reallocate resources, or implement corrective measures.

3.4 Lean Six Sigma in Cost Control

Lean Six Sigma Principles:

Combining Lean principles focused on efficiency with Six Sigma methodologies for quality improvement, Lean Six Sigma aims to eliminate waste, reduce defects, and enhance overall operational effectiveness.

Key Concepts:

1. Identifying Waste: Lean principles categorize various forms of waste, such as overproduction, unnecessary inventory, and inefficient processes.

2. Continuous Improvement: Six Sigma emphasizes a data-driven approach to identify and eliminate defects, driving ongoing process enhancement.

Practical Example:

A manufacturing company implementing Lean Six Sigma identifies a bottleneck in its production line, leading to delays and excess inventory. By streamlining the process and implementing quality control measures, the company reduces waste and ensures a smoother production flow, ultimately lowering costs.

In summary, this Chapter elucidates essential cost control strategies. From the proactive planning of budgeting and forecasting to the precision of activity-based costing, the diagnostic power of variance analysis, and the transformative potential of Lean Six Sigma, businesses can leverage these strategies to navigate the intricacies of cost control and enhance their overall financial health.

Chapter 4: Technology in Cost Management

In the contemporary business landscape, the integration of technology has become a pivotal force in reshaping how organizations approach cost management. Chapter 4 explores the role of technology in cost control, highlighting the impact of Enterprise Resource Planning (ERP) systems, the automation of processes, and the application of data analytics for cost optimization.

4.1 ERP Systems for Cost Control

Understanding ERP Systems:

Enterprise Resource Planning (ERP) systems are comprehensive software solutions that integrate and streamline various business processes. These systems provide a centralized platform for managing core business functions such as finance, human resources, supply chain, and more.

Key Components of ERP in Cost Control:

1. Financial Modules: Enable real-time tracking of expenses, revenue, and financial performance.

2. Supply Chain Management: Enhance visibility into the procurement process, optimizing inventory levels and reducing costs.

3. Human Resources Integration: Streamline payroll and workforce management, contributing to overall cost efficiency.

Practical Example:

Consider a multinational corporation implementing an ERP system. The system seamlessly integrates data from different departments, allowing management to monitor real-time financial performance, identify cost trends, and make data-driven decisions. Through improved efficiency and transparency, the company gains a competitive edge in cost control.

4.2 Automation and AI Applications

Automation in Cost Management:

Automation involves the use of technology to perform tasks without human intervention. In cost management, automation streamlines routine processes, reduces manual errors, and enhances overall efficiency.

Applications in Cost Management:

1. Invoice Processing: Automated systems can process invoices, ensuring accuracy and timely payments.

2. Expense Reporting: Automation simplifies the tracking and approval of employee expenses, reducing administrative overhead.

3. Budgeting and Forecasting: AI-powered tools analyze historical data and market trends, providing more accurate predictions for budgeting purposes.

Practical Example:

An e-commerce company automates its inventory management processes using AI algorithms. By predicting demand patterns, the system optimizes stock levels, minimizing both excess inventory costs and the risk of stock outs. This not only improves cost control but also enhances customer satisfaction through better product availability.

4.3 Data Analytics for Cost Optimization

Role of Data Analytics in Cost Management:

Data analytics involves the systematic analysis of data to uncover insights, trends, and patterns. In cost management, leveraging data analytics allows organizations to make informed decisions, identify cost-saving opportunities, and continuously optimize their financial strategies.

Key Aspects of Data Analytics in Cost Optimization:

1. Predictive Analytics: Forecasting future cost trends based on historical data and market indicators.

2. Cost Attribution: Allocating costs to specific activities or products for a granular understanding of expenditure.

3. Performance Metrics: Utilizing Key Performance Indicators (KPIs) to measure and evaluate cost-control initiatives.

Practical Example:

A retail chain utilizes data analytics to analyze customer purchasing behavior. By understanding which products are driving the highest revenue and margins, the company can adjust pricing strategies and marketing efforts to maximize profitability. This data-driven approach contributes to efficient cost management and revenue optimization.

In essence, this Chapter illuminates the transformative influence of technology on cost control. From the comprehensive capabilities of ERP systems to the efficiency gains through automation and the strategic insights derived from data analytics, businesses can harness these technological advancements to not only manage costs effectively but also gain a competitive edge in today's dynamic business environment.

Chapter 5: Strategic Cost Reduction

Cost reduction is a critical aspect of financial management, and Chapter 5 delves into strategic approaches for minimizing expenses while maintaining operational effectiveness. This chapter explores methods for identifying cost-cutting opportunities, implementing cost reduction initiatives, and striking a balance between reducing costs and creating long-term value for the organization.

5.1 Identifying Cost-Cutting Opportunities

Comprehensive Cost Assessment:

Identifying cost-cutting opportunities requires a thorough examination of all aspects of the business. This involves assessing both direct and indirect costs across various departments and functions. Common areas for consideration include:

1. Operational Efficiency: Analyzing processes to identify redundancies and inefficiencies that contribute to unnecessary costs.

2. Supply Chain Optimization: Evaluating the supply chain for potential cost-saving opportunities, such as negotiating better deals with suppliers or consolidating orders.

3. Technology Utilization: Assessing the efficiency of current technologies and exploring cost-effective alternatives that enhance productivity.

Practical Example:

A manufacturing company reviews its production processes and identifies a substantial amount of waste in materials due to outdated machinery. By investing in newer, more efficient equipment, the company reduces material waste, leading to significant cost savings in the long run.

5.2 Implementing Cost Reduction Initiatives

Strategic Planning and Implementation:

Once cost-cutting opportunities are identified, the next step is to develop and implement initiatives that align with the organization's strategic goals. Key considerations include:

1. Prioritization: Identifying which cost-cutting initiatives will have the most substantial impact and prioritizing them based on urgency and potential return on investment.

2. Employee Involvement: Engaging employees in the cost reduction process, as they often have valuable insights into operational inefficiencies and potential improvements.

3. Communication: Transparently communicating the reasons behind cost reduction initiatives and outlining the expected benefits helps gain employee buy-in and support.

Practical Example:

A service-oriented business facing increased operating costs decides to implement a remote work policy. By reducing office space requirements and associated costs, the company not only cuts expenses but also enhances employee satisfaction and work-life balance.

5.3 Balancing Cost Reduction with Value Creation

Striking the Right Balance:

While cost reduction is essential, it's equally crucial to maintain a focus on creating value. A myopic approach solely centered on cutting costs can lead to diminished quality, reduced innovation, and a negative impact on employee morale. Striking the right balance involves:

1. Innovation and Investment: Identifying areas where strategic investments can lead to long-term savings or revenue generation.

2. Quality Maintenance: Ensuring that cost-cutting measures do not compromise the quality of products or services, maintaining customer satisfaction.

3. Employee Development: Investing in employee training and development to enhance skills and productivity, contributing to long-term value creation.

Practical Example:

A technology company implements a cost reduction strategy by outsourcing certain non-core functions. Simultaneously, it allocates funds for research and development, fostering innovation and maintaining a competitive edge in the market.

5.4 Monitoring and Adjusting Cost Reduction Strategies

Continuous Improvement:

Cost reduction is not a one-time event but an ongoing process that requires monitoring and adjustment. Regularly reviewing the effectiveness of implemented strategies and making necessary adjustments is crucial. Key aspects include:

1. Performance Metrics: Establishing key performance indicators (KPIs) to measure the success of cost reduction initiatives.

2. Feedback Mechanisms: Creating channels for feedback from employees and stakeholders to identify potential challenges or areas for improvement.

3. Flexibility: Adapting strategies based on changing market conditions, technological advancements, and organizational needs.

Practical Example:

An e-commerce company implements a cost reduction strategy by optimizing its digital marketing spend. By regularly analyzing the performance of different advertising channels and adjusting budgets based on ROI, the company ensures efficient resource allocation and maximizes cost savings.

5.5 Case Studies

Real-world Examples of Successful Cost Reduction:

Ford Motor Company (2006-2008): During a challenging period for the automotive industry, Ford implemented a comprehensive cost-cutting strategy, including plant closures, workforce reductions, and renegotiations with suppliers. This strategic approach helped Ford navigate the economic downturn and return to profitability.

Procter & Gamble (P&G): P&G embarked on a cost reduction initiative by streamlining its product portfolio, focusing on core brands, and implementing efficiency measures in its supply chain. This strategic move allowed P&G to enhance profitability while maintaining brand strength.

Lessons Learned from Cost Control Failures:

Kodak (Late 20th Century): Kodak failed to adapt to the digital photography revolution, resulting in significant financial challenges. The company's reluctance to invest in new technologies and diversify its product offerings contributed to its decline.

Blockbuster (Early 21st Century): Blockbuster, once a dominant force in the video rental industry, faced bankruptcy due to its inability to adapt to the shift towards online streaming. The company's resistance to embracing emerging technologies ultimately led to its downfall.

5.6 Future Trends in Business Cost Control

Emerging Technologies and Their Impact:

The future of cost control is closely tied to technological advancements. Key trends shaping the landscape include:

1. Blockchain Technology: Enhancing transparency and security in financial transactions, reducing the risk of fraud and errors.

2. Artificial Intelligence (AI): Enabling more sophisticated data analytics, predictive modeling, and automation for enhanced cost management.

3. Cloud Computing: Facilitating cost-effective access to advanced computing resources, allowing businesses to scale without significant infrastructure investments.

Sustainability and Cost Management:

As businesses increasingly prioritize sustainability, integrating environmentally conscious practices into cost management is becoming a prominent trend. This involves:

1. Green Supply Chain: Opting for suppliers with environmentally friendly practices and reducing the carbon footprint of the supply chain.

2. Energy Efficiency: Implementing technologies and processes that minimize energy consumption, resulting in long-term cost savings.

Adapting to Changing Business Environments:

Flexibility and adaptability are crucial in navigating evolving business landscapes. Key considerations include:

1. Remote Work Strategies: Continued exploration of remote work options to optimize operational costs and enhance employee flexibility.

2. Globalization Challenges: Assessing and mitigating risks associated with global supply chains, geopolitical factors, and economic uncertainties.

Chapter 5 concludes by emphasizing the dynamic nature of cost reduction strategies. It underscores the importance of a holistic approach that considers not only immediate cost-cutting measures but also long-term value creation and adaptability to emerging trends. Strategic cost reduction, when executed thoughtfully, positions organizations for resilience and sustained success in an ever-changing business environment.

Chapter 6: Best Practices in Cost Control

Cost control is not a static process; it requires ongoing evaluation and adaptation. Chapter 6 delves into the best practices that organizations can adopt to optimize their cost management strategies. From benchmarking and performance metrics to effective risk management and continuous improvement strategies, this chapter explores the nuanced approaches that contribute to sustained financial health.

6.1 Benchmarking and Performance Metrics

Benchmarking Overview:

Benchmarking involves comparing an organization's processes, products, or services against industry standards or best practices. It serves as a valuable tool for identifying areas of improvement and setting performance targets.

Types of Benchmarking:

1. Internal Benchmarking: Comparing performance metrics within different departments or units within the same organization.

2. Competitive Benchmarking: Assessing performance against direct competitors in the industry.

3. Functional Benchmarking: Analyzing processes or functions that are similar across different industries.

Key Performance Metrics:

Establishing and monitoring key performance indicators (KPIs) is essential for effective cost control. These metrics vary based on the industry and organizational goals but commonly include:

1. Cost-to-Income Ratio: Assessing the proportion of costs relative to revenue.

2. Return on Investment (ROI): Evaluating the profitability of investments or initiatives.

3. Operating Efficiency: Measuring how efficiently resources are utilized to produce goods or deliver services.

Practical Example:

A retail company uses competitive benchmarking to assess its inventory turnover rate against industry standards. By comparing its performance to that of similar retailers, the company identifies opportunities to streamline its inventory management processes, reducing carrying costs and improving overall efficiency.

6.2 Risk Management in Cost Control

Risk Identification and Assessment:

Effective risk management is integral to cost control. Organizations must identify and assess potential risks that could impact financial performance. This involves:

1. Risk Identification: Identifying internal and external factors that may pose threats to cost control, such as market fluctuations, supply chain disruptions, or regulatory changes.

2. Risk Assessment: Evaluating the likelihood and impact of identified risks to prioritize mitigation efforts.

Mitigation Strategies:

Implementing strategies to mitigate identified risks is crucial for minimizing their impact on costs. These strategies may include:

1. Diversification: Diversifying suppliers or markets to reduce dependence on a single source.

2. Insurance Coverage: Investing in insurance policies to mitigate financial losses due to unforeseen events.

3. Contingency Planning: Developing contingency plans to address potential disruptions and minimize their impact.

Practical Example:

A manufacturing company, recognizing the potential risks associated with fluctuations in raw material prices, establishes contracts with multiple suppliers. By diversifying its sources, the company mitigates the impact of sudden price increases from any single supplier, ensuring cost stability.

6.3 Continuous Improvement Strategies

Kaizen Philosophy:

Continuous improvement, rooted in the Kaizen philosophy, involves making incremental changes to processes over time. This approach fosters a culture of continuous learning and adaptation.

Key Principles of Continuous Improvement:

1. Employee Involvement: Encouraging employees at all levels to contribute ideas for process improvement.

2. Data-Driven Decision-Making: Utilizing data and analytics to identify areas for improvement and measure the impact of changes.

3. Iterative Approach: Implementing small, incremental changes and continuously reassessing their effectiveness.

Practical Example:

A technology company adopts continuous improvement strategies in its software development process. Through regular retrospectives and feedback loops, the development team identifies bottlenecks and inefficiencies. Small, iterative changes are implemented, leading to increased productivity and reduced development costs over time.

Chapter 6 underscores the importance of adopting best practices in cost control to enhance organizational performance and financial sustainability. From benchmarking and performance metrics that provide valuable insights into competitiveness, to risk management strategies that safeguard against unforeseen challenges, and continuous improvement methodologies that foster adaptability and innovation, these practices collectively contribute to a holistic and effective cost control framework.

Organizations that integrate these best practices into their operations are better positioned to navigate the complexities of the business landscape. As cost control becomes an integral part of organizational culture, it serves not only as a reactive measure to address immediate challenges but as a proactive strategy for long-term success and resilience.

Chapter 7: Case Studies

Case studies serve as real-world exemplars, providing invaluable insights into the application of cost control strategies within diverse business scenarios. This chapter examines specific cases, showcasing both successful implementations and lessons learned from failures. Through detailed analyses, we gain a deeper understanding of how organizations navigate challenges, make strategic decisions, and ultimately shape their financial destinies.

7.1 Real-world Examples of Successful Cost Control

Case Study 1: Toyota's Lean Manufacturing Revolution

Toyota's journey in implementing lean manufacturing principles stands as an epitome of successful cost control. In the 20th century, Toyota revolutionized the automotive industry by introducing the Toyota Production System (TPS), now widely known as lean manufacturing. Key principles include:

1. Just-in-Time (JIT) Inventory: Minimizing inventory levels to reduce carrying costs and improve efficiency.

2. Kaizen Continuous Improvement: Encouraging incremental improvements through employee involvement and empowerment.

3. Waste Reduction: Identifying and eliminating waste in all forms, including overproduction, defects, and unnecessary inventory.

Practical Application:

Imagine a scenario where a traditional manufacturing plant produces large batches of a product, leading to high inventory costs. By adopting lean principles, the plant transitions to JIT production, reducing inventory holding costs and improving overall efficiency. Continuous improvement initiatives further streamline processes, enhancing cost control while maintaining product quality.

Case Study 2: Amazon's Supply Chain Optimization

Amazon's success in e-commerce is closely tied to its mastery of supply chain optimization. The company leverages advanced technologies and data analytics to create a highly efficient and responsive supply chain. Key strategies include:

1. Predictive Analytics: Anticipating customer demand and optimizing inventory levels accordingly.

2. Fulfillment Centers: Strategically locating fulfillment centers for efficient order processing and timely deliveries.

3. Robotics and Automation: Incorporating robotics and automation to streamline warehouse operations and reduce labor costs.

Practical Application:

Consider a traditional retailer facing challenges with inventory management and order fulfillment. Inspired by Amazon's approach, the retailer invests in predictive analytics and automation. By accurately predicting demand and automating certain warehouse processes, the retailer minimizes excess inventory costs and achieves faster order fulfillment, enhancing customer satisfaction.

7.2 Lessons Learned from Cost Control Failures

Case Study 3: Kodak's Digital Transformation Failure

Kodak's failure to adapt to the digital photography era serves as a cautionary tale. Despite pioneering film-based photography, Kodak struggled to embrace digital technology, leading to financial decline. Key lessons include:

1. Lack of Innovation: Failing to invest in and adapt to emerging technologies can lead to obsolescence.

2. Inflexibility: Resisting change and holding onto traditional business models can hinder long-term viability.

3. Failure to Diversify: Over-reliance on a single product or technology leaves a company vulnerable to market shifts.

Practical Application:

Imagine a tech company heavily invested in a legacy software product. Learning from Kodak's experience, the company proactively explores emerging technologies and invests in research and development. By diversifying its product portfolio and staying innovative, the company mitigates the risk of becoming obsolete in a rapidly changing industry.

Case Study 4: Blockbuster's Resistance to Streaming

Blockbuster's reluctance to adapt to the rise of online streaming is another example of cost control failure. As streaming services gained popularity, Blockbuster's brick-and-mortar rental model became outdated. Key lessons include:

1. Failure to Anticipate Trends: Ignoring emerging trends and customer preferences can lead to market irrelevance.

2. Resistance to Technology: Failing to embrace technological advancements can result in a loss of competitive advantage.

3. Inability to Pivot: Being inflexible in business models can lead to missed opportunities for reinvention.

Practical Application:

An entertainment company, witnessing the shift towards digital streaming, chooses to invest in an online streaming platform. By adapting to changing consumer behaviors and embracing technology, the company not only retains its customer base but also gains a competitive edge in the evolving market.

7.3 Key Takeaways from Case Studies

1. Adaptability is Paramount: Successful organizations demonstrate a willingness to adapt to changing landscapes, whether through embracing new technologies or evolving business models.

2. Innovation Drives Success: The ability to innovate, whether in processes, products, or services, is a key factor in long-term success.

3. Diversification Mitigates Risks: Businesses that diversify their offerings and revenue streams are better equipped to weather industry shifts and economic uncertainties.

4. Customer-Centric Approaches: Understanding and responding to customer needs are pivotal in sustaining competitiveness and relevance.

5. Continuous Improvement is a Journey: Organizations committed to continuous improvement foster a culture of learning, adaptability, and resilience.

7.4 Future Trends in Case Studies

Emerging Technologies Shaping Case Studies:

1. Blockchain and Transparency: Future case studies may highlight the integration of blockchain technology for enhanced transparency in financial transactions and supply chain management.

2. Artificial Intelligence (AI) Applications: Case studies may showcase AI-driven analytics providing deeper insights into cost patterns and predictive modeling.

3. Sustainability in Action: As sustainability gains prominence, future cases may explore how organizations integrate environmentally conscious practices into their cost control strategies.

The Role of Case Studies in Learning:

1. Educational Value: Case studies offer practical lessons that go beyond theoretical knowledge, providing a bridge between academic concepts and real-world application.

2. Decision-Making Insights: Analyzing how organizations faced challenges and made decisions provides valuable insights into effective decision-making processes.

3. Benchmarking Opportunities: Case studies serve as benchmarks for organizations seeking to enhance their cost control strategies, offering inspiration and cautionary tales.

This Chapter draws to a close with a profound appreciation for the richness and diversity encapsulated within case studies. These real-world narratives, whether illustrating triumphs or cautionary tales, provide a dynamic framework for understanding the complexities of cost control in a constantly evolving business landscape. As organizations continue to navigate challenges and opportunities, case studies stand as invaluable repositories of knowledge, offering insights that extend beyond the pages of textbooks and into the practical realms of strategic decision-making and financial stewardship.

Chapter 8: Future Trends in Business Cost Control

As the business landscape evolves, organizations are compelled to anticipate and adapt to emerging trends in cost control. Chapter 8 delves into the future of cost management, exploring how technological advancements, sustainability considerations, and the ability to navigate changing business environments will shape the strategies employed by successful organizations. Practical examples illustrate how forward-thinking companies are already aligning with these future trends to gain a competitive edge.

8.1 Emerging Technologies and Their Impact

1. Blockchain Technology:

Future Application:

Blockchain's decentralized and transparent nature holds the potential to transform financial transactions and supply chain management. Imagine a scenario where a company utilizes blockchain to create an unalterable record of transactions in its supply chain. This not only enhances transparency but also mitigates the risk of fraud and ensures the authenticity of goods.

2. Artificial Intelligence (AI) Applications:

Future Application:

The integration of AI in cost control is poised to revolutionize data analytics and decision-making. Imagine a company employing AI-driven predictive analytics to forecast future cost trends. By analyzing vast datasets, the system can provide accurate predictions, enabling proactive cost management strategies and reducing reliance on reactive measures.

3. Cloud Computing:

Future Application:

Cloud computing continues to play a pivotal role in cost-effective access to advanced computing resources. A future application might involve a company transitioning its entire data infrastructure to the cloud, reducing the need for extensive on-premise hardware and associated maintenance costs. This shift not only enhances scalability but also provides a cost-efficient solution.

8.2 Sustainability and Cost Management

1. Green Supply Chain:

Future Application:

The integration of sustainability considerations into the supply chain is gaining prominence. A future scenario might involve a manufacturing company actively seeking suppliers with environmentally friendly practices. By embracing a green supply chain, the company not only aligns with sustainability goals but also potentially reduces costs associated with waste and energy consumption.

2. Energy Efficiency:

Future Application:

Companies are increasingly exploring energy-efficient technologies to reduce costs and environmental impact. Imagine a business investing in state-of-the-art equipment that consumes less energy in its manufacturing processes. This not only aligns with sustainability goals but also results in long-term cost savings through reduced energy expenses.

8.3 Adapting to Changing Business Environments

1. Remote Work Strategies:

Future Application:

The trend of remote work is expected to persist, and organizations will need to adapt their cost control strategies accordingly. A future application might involve a company embracing remote work on a more permanent basis, reducing costs associated with office space, utilities, and commuting allowances. This shift not only cuts operational costs but also enhances employee satisfaction and work-life balance.

2. Globalization Challenges:

Future Application:

As businesses navigate global uncertainties, future cost control strategies might involve a more careful evaluation of geopolitical risks. Companies may diversify suppliers or establish contingency plans to mitigate the impact of geopolitical events. This proactive approach helps ensure stability in the supply chain and minimizes potential disruptions.

8.4 Case Studies on Future Trends

Case Study 1: Implementing Blockchain in Supply Chain Management

Context:

A manufacturing company adopts blockchain technology to enhance transparency and traceability in its supply chain.

Implementation:

The company integrates blockchain to create an immutable record of transactions from raw material sourcing to product delivery. This not only provides real-time visibility but also reduces the risk of counterfeit products entering the supply chain.

Result:

By leveraging blockchain, the company not only strengthens its commitment to sustainability but also enhances its ability to track and optimize costs throughout the supply chain.

Case Study 2: AI-Driven Predictive Analytics for Cost Forecasting

Context:

A technology company embraces AI-driven predictive analytics to forecast future cost trends and proactively manage expenses.

Implement few machine learning algorithms, the company analyzes historical cost data, market trends, and external factors to generate accurate predictions. This enables the organization to make informed decisions and adjust cost **control strategies in anticipation of future challenges.**

Result:

The company gains a competitive edge by staying ahead of cost fluctuations, making strategic decisions based on data-driven insights, and optimizing resource allocation for enhanced financial performance.

Case Study 3: Green Supply Chain Initiatives for Cost Savings

Context:

A retail company prioritizes sustainability by integrating green practices into its supply chain.

Implementation:

The company collaborates with suppliers who adhere to environmentally friendly practices. Additionally, it explores energy-efficient transportation options and packaging materials, reducing the overall environmental impact of its operations.

Result:

The dual benefit of sustainability and cost savings is realized as the company establishes itself as a socially responsible brand. Reduced waste and energy consumption contribute to long-term financial gains.

8.5 Key Takeaways from Future Trends

1. Technological Integration is Inevitable: Organizations must embrace emerging technologies such as blockchain, AI, and cloud computing to stay competitive in cost management.

2. Sustainability is a Strategic Imperative: The intertwining of sustainability goals with cost control strategies not only aligns with societal expectations but also brings about tangible cost savings.

3. Flexibility is Essential: Future-proofing cost control strategies requires adaptability to remote work trends, geopolitical shifts, and other evolving business environments.

4. Data Driven Decision-Making: The role of data analytics, powered by AI, will be central in making proactive and informed decisions for effective cost control.

This Chapter concludes with a forward-looking perspective on the future trends that will shape the landscape of cost control. As organizations navigate the complexities of emerging technologies, sustainability considerations, and evolving business environments, the ability to proactively adapt and integrate these trends into their cost management strategies will be pivotal. By learning from practical examples and case studies, businesses can position themselves to thrive in a future where cost control is not just a reactive measure but a strategic and dynamic component of overall financial stewardship.

Chapter 9: Ethical Considerations in Cost Control

In the realm of business cost control, ethical considerations are paramount. Chapter 9 explores the ethical dimensions associated with managing costs, emphasizing the importance of integrity, transparency, and responsible financial stewardship. This chapter delves into the complexities of ethical decision-making in cost control and provides practical examples to illustrate the application of ethical principles.

9.1 Ethics in Cost Control: An Overview

1. Integrity in Financial Reporting:

Ethical Principle:

Maintaining integrity in financial reporting involves providing accurate, transparent, and unbiased information about an organization's financial performance.

Practical Example:

Consider a scenario where a company is facing financial challenges, and there is pressure to present a more positive financial picture to stakeholders. Ethical leaders within the organization resist the temptation to manipulate financial statements and instead focus on addressing the root causes of financial difficulties transparently.

2. Fair Treatment of Employees:

Ethical Principle:

Ensuring fair treatment of employees in cost control involves making decisions that consider the well-being, job security, and fair compensation of employees.

Practical Example:

Imagine a company implementing cost-cutting measures due to economic challenges. Ethical leadership involves transparent communication with employees, exploring alternatives to layoffs, and ensuring that the burden of cost reductions is shared equitably across the organization.

3. Honesty in Supplier Relationships:

Ethical Principle:

Maintaining honesty in supplier relationships involves fair and transparent dealings, avoiding deceptive practices, and upholding contractual agreements.

Practical Example:

A company negotiating with suppliers for cost reductions ethically discloses its financial constraints and collaboratively explores ways to reduce costs without compromising the fair compensation of suppliers. Open communication fosters trust and long term partnerships.

9.2 Ethical Decision-Making Frameworks

1. Utilitarianism:

Framework Overview:

Utilitarianism evaluates ethical decisions based on the principle of maximizing overall happiness or utility. Decisions are considered ethical if they result in the greatest benefit for the greatest number.

Practical Example:

A manufacturing company is considering outsourcing certain operations to reduce costs. Utilitarian ethical analysis involves assessing the overall impact on employees, customers, and stakeholders. If outsourcing leads to greater benefits for the majority, it aligns with a utilitarian framework.

2. Deontology:

Framework Overview:

Deontology emphasizes adherence to moral principles and duties, irrespective of the consequences. Decisions are deemed ethical if they align with established moral rules or principles.

Practical Example:

A company committed to fair labor practices adheres to deontological principles when making decisions about employee compensation. Even if reducing wages could bring short-term cost savings, ethical leaders prioritize upholding the moral duty to provide fair and just compensation.

3. Virtue Ethics:

Framework Overview:

Virtue ethics focuses on the development of virtuous character traits. Decisions are considered ethical if they align with virtues such as honesty, integrity, and fairness.

Practical Example:

In a cost-cutting scenario, a leader guided by virtue ethics prioritizes open communication and fairness. This leader ensures that decisions reflect virtuous qualities, fostering a corporate culture based on ethical principles.

9.3 Challenges in Ethical Cost Control

1. Short-Term vs. Long-Term Trade-offs:

Challenge:

Balancing short-term cost reduction goals with long-term ethical considerations poses a challenge. The pressure to achieve immediate financial results may conflict with the ethical obligation to maintain integrity and fairness.

Practical Example:

A company facing financial difficulties may be tempted to cut corners on employee benefits to achieve quick cost savings. Ethical leaders navigate this challenge by considering the long-term impact on employee morale, productivity, and the company's reputation.

2. Globalization and Ethical Standards:

Challenge:

Operating in a globalized environment introduces challenges related to varying ethical standards and practices across different regions. Ethical decisions must navigate cultural nuances and legal frameworks.

Practical Example:

A multinational corporation expanding into a new market must consider local ethical norms and legal requirements. Ethical leaders engage in cross-cultural training and adapt policies to align with local expectations while upholding global ethical standards.

9.4 Best Practices for Ethical Cost Control

1. Establishing a Code of Ethics:

Best Practice:

Organizations committed to ethical cost control establish a comprehensive code of ethics. This code provides clear guidelines for ethical decision-making and serves as a reference for employees at all levels.

Practical Application:

A company develops a code of ethics that explicitly outlines principles related to cost control, emphasizing transparency, fairness, and integrity. This code guides employees when faced with ethical dilemmas in financial decision-making.

2. Ethical Leadership Training:

Best Practice

Investing in ethical leadership training ensures that leaders understand the ethical implications of their decisions. Training programs focus on promoting ethical awareness, decision-making skills, and the importance of leading by example.

Practical Application:

A company conducts regular training sessions for its leadership team on ethical decision-making in cost control. This training emphasizes case studies, role-playing scenarios, and discussions to enhance leaders' ethical reasoning skills.

9.5 Case Studies on Ethical Cost Control

Case Study 1: Transparency in Financial Reporting

Context:

A publicly traded company faces financial challenges and is under pressure to present a more positive financial image to shareholders.

Ethical Decision:

The leadership team chooses transparency over manipulation, providing an accurate portrayal of the company's financial situation. They communicate openly about the challenges and implement cost-control measures responsibly.

Result:

While the immediate impact may include a temporary decrease in stock value, the company earns trust from shareholders and stakeholders. Over the long term, this commitment to transparency enhances the company's reputation and sustainability.

Case Study 2: Fair Treatment of Employees in Cost-Cutting Measures

Context:

An organization experiences economic downturns, leading to the need for cost-cutting measures.

Ethical Decision:

The leadership prioritizes fair treatment of employees by exploring alternatives to layoffs, implementing temporary pay reductions for all employees, including executives, and maintaining open communication throughout the process.

Result:

While the cost-cutting measures impact employees, the ethical approach fosters loyalty, employee morale remains higher, and the organization retains a positive employer brand. The long-term benefits include a more committed workforce and potential for increased productivity.

9.6 Future Considerations in Ethical Cost Control

1. AI and Ethical Decision-Making:

Future Trend:

As AI becomes more integrated into decision-making processes, organizations will need to ensure that AI algorithms align with ethical principles. This involves designing algorithms that prioritize

fairness, transparency, and the well-being of stakeholders.

Practical Application:

A company adopting AI-driven cost control tools ensures that the algorithms consider the ethical implications

Chapter 10: Innovation in Business Cost Control

Innovation is a driving force in business evolution, and Chapter 10 explores how organizations can harness innovative approaches to enhance cost control strategies. From leveraging technology and process optimization to fostering a culture of continuous improvement, this chapter delves into the dynamic intersection of innovation and cost management. Practical examples illustrate how forward-thinking companies have successfully integrated innovation into their cost control initiatives.

10.1 Technology-Driven Innovations

1. Automation and Robotics:

Innovation Overview:

Automation and robotics have the potential to revolutionize cost control by streamlining processes, reducing labor costs, and enhancing efficiency.

Practical Example:

A manufacturing company adopts robotic automation in its production line, significantly reducing labor costs, minimizing errors, and improving overall operational efficiency. The upfront investment in robotics yields long-term cost savings and increased productivity.

2. Advanced Data Analytics:

Innovation Overview:

Utilizing advanced data analytics enables organizations to gain deeper insights into cost patterns, identify opportunities for optimization, and make informed decisions.

Practical Example:

A retail company employs predictive analytics to analyze customer purchasing behavior. By understanding trends and demand patterns, the company optimizes inventory levels, reducing carrying costs and preventing stock outs, ultimately improving cost-effectiveness.

3. Cloud-Based Solutions:

Innovation Overview:

Cloud computing offers scalable and cost-effective solutions for data storage, processing, and collaborative work environments.

Practical Example:

An expanding startup transitions its entire IT infrastructure to cloud-based solutions. This not only eliminates the need for significant upfront hardware investments but also provides flexibility, scalability, and efficient resource utilization, leading to substantial cost savings.

10.2 Process Optimization and Continuous Improvement

1. Lean Management Principles:

Innovation Overview:

Lean management principles focus on eliminating waste, improving efficiency, and enhancing overall value in processes.

Practical Example:

A service-oriented business applies lean principles to streamline its customer service processes. By identifying and eliminating inefficiencies, the company reduces operational costs while improving the quality and speed of customer interactions.

2. Agile Methodology:

Innovation Overview:

Agile methodology, commonly used in software development, emphasizes adaptability, collaboration, and iterative improvements.

Practical Example:

An IT department adopts agile methodology for project management. By breaking down large projects into smaller, manageable tasks and regularly reassessing priorities, the team improves project efficiency, reduces delays, and optimizes resource utilization.

10.3 Cultural Innovation and Employee Engagement

1. Employee-Driven Innovation:

Innovation Overview:

Fostering a culture of innovation that encourages employees to contribute ideas for process improvement and cost control.

Practical Example:

An organization implements an employee suggestion program where staff members are encouraged to propose innovative ideas for cost reduction. This not only taps into the collective intelligence of the workforce but also instills a sense of ownership and engagement.

2. Training and Skill Development:

Innovation Overview:

Investing in training and skill development ensures that employees are equipped to embrace new technologies and contribute to innovative cost control strategies.

Practical Example:

A manufacturing company invests in training programs to upskill its workforce in the use of advanced manufacturing technologies. This not only enhances employee capabilities but also leads to improved operational efficiency and cost savings.

10.4 Case Studies on Innovative Cost Control

Case Study 1: Amazon's Fulfillment Center Robotics

Context:

Amazon, a global e-commerce giant, innovates its order fulfillment process through the extensive use of robotics in its warehouses.

Innovation Implementation:

Amazon introduces robotic systems to automate tasks such as picking, packing, and transporting goods within its fulfillment centers. This reduces the need for manual labor, improves order accuracy, and accelerates the order fulfillment process.

Result:

The integration of robotics not only enhances operational efficiency but also contributes to significant cost savings in labor, reducing fulfillment costs per unit and allowing Amazon to scale its operations efficiently.

Case Study 2: Toyota's Production System

Context:

Toyota revolutionizes manufacturing with its Toyota Production System (TPS), a pioneering example of lean management principles.

Innovation Implementation:

Toyota adopts lean principles to eliminate waste, reduce inventory, and improve production efficiency. The company introduces concepts such as just-in-time (JIT) inventory and continuous improvement (Kaizen) to optimize its manufacturing processes.

Result:

The Toyota Production System becomes a benchmark for efficiency in the automotive industry. Toyota achieves cost savings by minimizing excess inventory, improving production flow, and enhancing overall operational efficiency.

10.5 Challenges in Innovative Cost Control

1. Initial Investment Costs:

Challenge:

Implementing innovative technologies or processes often requires significant upfront investments, which can be a barrier for some organizations.

Practical Consideration:

Organizations need to conduct a thorough cost-benefit analysis to assess the long-term savings and improvements in efficiency that innovative solutions can bring. This helps justify the initial investment and demonstrate the value of the innovation.

2. Resistance to Change:

Challenge:

Employees and stakeholders may resist changes brought about by innovation, leading to challenges in implementation.

Practical Consideration:

Effective communication, training programs, and involving employees in the innovation process help mitigate resistance. Organizations should create a culture that values continuous improvement and fosters an understanding of the benefits of innovation in cost control.

10.6 Future Trends in Innovative Cost Control

1. Integration of Artificial Intelligence (AI):

Future Trend:

AI is expected to play a more significant role in cost control, particularly in areas such as predictive analytics, process automation, and decision-making support.

Practical Consideration:

Organizations should explore how AI applications can be integrated into their cost control strategies. This may involve leveraging AI-powered tools for data analysis, forecasting, and identifying optimization opportunities.

2. Sustainability-Driven Innovation:

Future Trend:

The intersection of innovation and sustainability is likely to become more pronounced, with organizations innovating to reduce environmental impact and align with sustainable practices.

Practical Consideration:

Companies should explore sustainable innovations in their products, processes, and supply chains. This includes adopting eco-friendly technologies and practices that contribute to both cost reduction and environmental responsibility.

This chapter concludes with the recognition that innovation is not just a buzzword but a fundamental aspect of effective cost control. Organizations that embrace innovative approaches, whether through technology adoption, process optimization, or fostering a culture of continuous improvement, position themselves for long-term success. By learning from practical examples and case studies, businesses can understand the transformative power of innovation in shaping more efficient, adaptive, and cost-effective operations in the dynamic landscape of modern business.

CONCLUSION

In conclusion, the Business Cost Control System book is an invaluable resource for businesses seeking to optimize their financial performance and drive sustainable growth. By providing comprehensive insights and practical strategies, this book equips organizations with the tools they need to effectively manage and control costs.

With the ever-increasing complexity of the business landscape, cost control has become a critical factor for success. This book offers a roadmap to navigate the intricacies of cost management, empowering businesses to identify inefficiencies, streamline processes, and make informed decisions that positively impact their bottom line.

The author's expertise and deep understanding of cost control principles shine through every chapter, offering real-world examples and case studies that bring concepts to life. From budgeting and forecasting to analyzing cost drivers and implementing cost-saving initiatives, this book covers a wide range of topics, providing actionable insights that can be applied across industries and business sizes.

By implementing the strategies outlined in this book, businesses can gain a competitive edge, enhance profitability, and ensure long-term financial stability. The Business Cost Control System book is a must-read for executives, managers, and entrepreneurs who are committed to achieving financial excellence and driving their organizations towards sustainable success.

Thanks for Reading